C

Learn C # Programming with the Ultimate Crash Course for Beginners in no Time!

Introduction

I want to thank you and congratulate you for downloading the book, *"C#: Learn C# Programming with the Ultimate Crash Course for Beginners in No Time!"*

This book contains proven steps and strategies on how to start writing programs with C# in the soonest time possible!

If you have prior knowledge about the world of *C++* programming, then you may find familiar terms and code structure with *C#* (pronounced as *See Sharp*). It works with Microsoft *.NET* framework and was initially designed to be the answer to *Java*. Today, both are being used extensively by companies and are also a friendly language for beginners.

Here are some of the essential lessons you will find inside:

- *Comprehending the C# Program Structure*

- *The Coding Conventions for C#*

- *Mastering Variables and Data Types*

- *Getting Using Input and Using Type Conversions*

- *Arithmetic, Conditional, Relational, and Logical Operators*

- *Using Flow Control Statements*

- *Generating Random Numbers*

- *And much more!*

Thanks again for downloading this book. I hope you enjoy it!

Chapter 1 – Getting Started

In this Chapter:

**Brief Introduction to C#

**Downloading a Free IDE and Compiler

**The Basic Terms of C#

If you are reading this book, then you are probably:

- A student

- A hobbyist

- A professional in need of a reference

If you are completely new to the world of programming, then you should know that you need two things before you can start. To be specific, you need to install an *Integrated Development Environment* or IDE so you can write your code and a *compiler* to build your codes into a runnable piece of application.

Usually, these two come bundled together. If you are a student and currently has a subject for C#, then you should probably ask for a copy of these two from your instructor. Otherwise, you need to purchase or download an IDE from the internet.

For you to get started right away, you can choose from any of the free IDEs that include C# functionality below:

- **Microsoft Visual Studio Express –** www.visualstudio.com

- **MonoDevelop –** www.monodevelop.com

- **SharpDevelop –** www.icsharpcode.net/opensource/SD

Take note that the interfaces and shortcut commands for each IDE will vary. This is why the instructions of this book when it comes to accessing certain functions will be generalized, but the codes themselves should be exactly the same. Go ahead and download the one you prefer.

If you are using Mac OS or Linux, then you may want to choose the cross-platform *MonoDevelop*. This particular IDE is feature-rich and has an interface that is very easy to get into. However, if you want an IDE that is lightweight, then you should go for *SharpDevelop*. Finally, you should choose *Visual Studio Express* in case you are interested in the added features of upgrading to *Visual Studio Professional* later on. Bear in mind that the programs listed above already come with compilers, so it is no longer necessary to look for one. After downloading your software, then you are ready to get started with coding.

The Basic Terms of C#

If you have never programmed before, a lot of the terms used in the following chapters such as statements, parameters, expressions, methods, and classes will definitely be confusing to you. Here is a quick reference guide for the basic terms in the world of C# programming:

- **Class** – A *class* is a group of methods and variables which define the behavior of instances, namely *objects* in object-oriented programming.

- **Method** – A method in C# is similar to a function in C++. Methods contain specific procedures for a class. Throughout the lessons this book, many methods or functions will be used such as `Console.WriteLine`, `Convert`, and so on.

- **Object** – Objects are instances that apply the specifications set by a class.

- **Statement** – Statements are the building blocks of any program. Declarations, expressions, iterations, initiations, and a number of other actions within a program are statements.

- **Operators** – C# uses a lot of operator symbols that are similar to those useable in C++. Operators are used to perform arithmetic and logical operations between different data types. Some of the operators in C# are **increment and decrement** (-- and ++), **multiplicative** (*, /, and %), **additive** (+ and -), and several others for logical and conditional expressions.

- **Variables** – Variables are essentially just containers for specific pieces of data, which can have different types such as *integral, floating point, decimal, Boolean, nullable,* and *textual.* Remember that specific data types only permit specific values.

- **Expressions** – Expressions can include operators, variables, method invocations, and values. Depending on what an expression consists of, it may be classified as an *invocation expression, query expression, literal expressions,* and *simple name expressions.* There are also expressions known as *Lambda expressions,* which are used only for *Language-Integrated Query* or LINQ.

Chapter 2 – The Program Structure

In this Chapter:

**The Hello World Program

**Understanding the C# Program Structure

**Basic Guidelines for Syntax (The Coding Conventions)

Sometimes, the best way to learn something you are clueless about is to jump into the action. If you have studied other programming languages before, then you probably encountered the *Hello World* program that every beginner knows. It is the simplest of all programs with the sole function of printing the words *Hello World* and nothing else.

To help you understand the *program structure* of C#, let us begin with the Hello World program as an example. Here is what the Hello World program looks like in C#:

```csharp
using System;

namespace Test

/* The two lines above are Namespace
Declarations */
{
```

```
/* Just like in C++, brackets are used to
segregate classes and methods */


    class MainClass
    {

        public static void Main (string[]
args)
        {
            Console.WriteLine ("Hello
World!");

            /* Feel free to edit the texts
            between the parentheses and
            quotation marks */

        }
    }

}
```

Before anything else, remember that anything written between '/*' and '*/' are seen by the compiler as the *comments*. They do not affect the program in any way and are only included by developers for organization, so you can write anything you like within them. Pay attention to the comments found in the code examples throughout this book as they will denote something useful.

Remember that the Hello World program is a *console application,*

Namespace Declaration

At the beginning of the program, notice how the namespace *system* is declared (`using System;`). *System* is essentially a collection of codes that is called upon by the Hello World program. Using namespaces is generally considered as a good habit for developers since it prevents issues within the program such as *name clashes*.

Take note that if the *System* namespace is not used in this program, the line `Console.WriteLine` will have to be written as `System.Console.WriteLine`. But if you use the namespace declaration for System, then you do not have to include System whenever you write a `Console.WriteLine` function.

After declaring the System namespace, the program now declares a new namespace called *Test* (`namespace Test`). Remember that Test can be any word that will describe your program. You can use something like *MyProgram* or *HelloWorld* just for personalization, but it will not have an effect on the program.

Class Declaration

Next is the *class declaration* (`class MainClass`). Just like the declaration of the Test namespace, you can use any word you like to label this class. In C# programming, namespaces contain multiple classes that, in turn, contain different methods. These terms will be explained as you go through this book. While using the same label for your namespace and class will work with the Hello World program, you should never use similar names when writing other programs.

The Main Method

The next statement, `public static void Main (string[] args),` initiates a *method* in the Hello World program. In this particular line, the *Main* method was initialized. Always remember that the Main method is called the *entry point* of C# programs because it is called first whenever the program starts. The words public and static are both *modifiers* while void indicates that this method has no return value. The *public* modifier basically allows the method to be called from external locations outside the class. *Static,* on the other hand, makes the method a member of the class itself and not a particular object of the class.

Finally, the `(string[] args)` defines the *parameters* to be included for the main method. This also allows arguments and values to be passed over to this method. But for a program like

Hello World that does not use command line arguments, you can leave the spaces between the parentheses blank and define the main method only with `public static void Main ()`.

The next statement, which is included in the main method, uses the `Console.WriteLine` function. This is the basic output function for C#. Whenever it is called, it will print the text contained between the parentheses and quotation marks in the console application.

The C# Coding Conventions

Outside the required syntax for a functional C# program, there are other standards or *conventions* being followed by programmers. More specifically, there are the C# coding conventions set by Microsoft to serve as guidelines for related documentation. These, according to the programming community, are the good practices that you should start adapting to as soon as you begin.

While they sometime do not have a direct effect on the program itself, it can help make other things such as debugging, modifying, and optimizing easier. For example, it is entirely possible to write a program in a lateral manner. But it is considered as a bad practice because it greatly reduces the readability of your code. As much as possible, programmers are encouraged to write *1 statement* per line.

There are several other guidelines that professional programmers follow that are related to almost every aspect of C#. But for beginners, here are the essential practices you should always remember as you learn the art of C# programming:

- Do not write anything in the same line as curly braces

- Do not write anything in the same line as comments

- Focus on the 1:1 rule; write only *one* declaration or statement in a single line

- Always use indentations

- If lines are not indented automatically by the IDE, use tab to indent them yourself

- Make sure paired curly braces are aligned (opening and closing)

Chapter 3 – All About Data

In this Chapter:

**The Basic Input for C#*

**Introduction to Variables and Data Types*

**The Different Methods of Declaring Variables and Output*

The Hello World program described in the previous chapter is a complete program in a sense that it accomplishes what it was written to do. Unfortunately, it is not meant for something more than just outputting information. Remember that programming languages are invented so humans can communicate with machines. But what you have done so far with the Hello World program is to write something that will do the exact same thing over and over again; without the participation of the *end-user*.

The Basic Input

There is also *one issue* that may arise with the Hello World program, or at least, the *version* of the Hello World program in the previous chapter. In some compilers, running the program will only briefly flash the console application before it closes almost immediately. This is because there is *nothing* else that follows after the `Console.WriteLine` function. Once it does its job, a program will naturally terminate.

A quick and easy way to prevent this is to tell your program to *wait* for user input before ending its life cycle, which can be done by adding the function:

```
Console.ReadKey ();
```

You can add this line after the `Console.WriteLine` function within the Main method, meaning you should not add it *after* the very next curly brace after said function. For now, you can leave the space for parameters (between the parentheses) empty since you will not need them.

Go ahead and try running the new program. You should now notice that the program *waits* before any key is pressed before quitting. Take note that for IDEs like MonoDevelop, the user is prompted a message like *press any key to continue*. When a key is pressed, it will automatically be printed in the console application window.

Telling the program to await user input is just the tip of the iceberg when it comes to user input in C# development. The next step is to learn how to *store* user input into variables and somehow utilize that information. But first, you should learn how to *declare* variables.

Declaring Variables

As mentioned in the first chapter, variables are basically any name that contains a specific data type. Variables are used for the purpose of storing user input. But before a variable can be used, it must first be *declared*. The same rule applies for every other programming language in existence.

To declare a variable, you need to use the following syntax:

```
var MyVar = "insert value here";
```

Bear in mind that *MyVar* can be replaced with anything you want to name your variable. Just remember that C# is case-sensitive, so it is best to take note of capitalizations when naming variables. The same goes for naming classes and methods.

Next is the basic *assignment operator* (=) which allows you to set a value for your variable. Take note that no *data type* is specified if you are to declare variables using only the var function. Instead, the data type will be automatically determined depending on what kind of data you associate when you declare the variable. This is why you cannot declare an undefined variable using this method.

However, you do not really need to assign a value to variables as soon as the program starts. With this being said, you can simply declare a variable by omitting the assignment operator and shortening your declaration to:

```
<Data type> MyVar;
```

But first, what exactly are data types and how do they differ? First of all, there are three categories encompassing different data types; *value types, reference types,* and *pointer types.* For the rest of this book, much of the focus will be invested on value data types. These are the data types that are usually embedded as values to variables.

The Data Types List

There are *13* total data types. But we will only be expounding and using a few of them throughout this book. Remember that there are *default values* to these data types, which are used in case you do not set the value yourself when declaring variables with them:

- **Boolean (bool)** – The Boolean or *bool* data type only has two possible values; *true* or *false.* This is extremely convenient for creating conditions. The default value for this data type is *false.* Take note that unlike in C++, the Boolean values in C# do not have numerical values. This means true is not equal to 1 and false is not equal to 0.

- **Character (char)** – A character or *char* data type is represented by a single Unicode character or simply just *text.* Remember that this particular data type uses only a single character, as opposed to the *string* data type. The default value for this data type is '\0'.

- **Integer (int)** – For basic programming purposes, you will be relying mostly on the integer or *int* data type when dealing with numbers. The int data type is considered as a *signed integer,* which are identified by computers using *2s complement.* The default value for the int data type is 0.

- **String (string)** – The string data type is basically a sequence of characters. A string may also contain numerals. This is ideal when storing information such as names, passwords, words, and basically any other sequence that uses alphanumeric characters.

- **Decimal (decimal)** – Remember that other data types, namely *float* and *double,* can be used with integers that have precise decimal values. However, for most numerical concepts in the human language (money, measurements, etc.), it is always simpler to use the decimal data type. For artifacts or values used for the sole purpose of calculations within the program, sometimes float or double is more apt. The default value for a decimal type is *0.0M.*

The data types that will not be expounded on in this book are the following:

- **Float (float)** – The float data type contains 32-bit floating-point values. It is basically short for *floating point,* which refers to a decimal point somewhere within the digits. Float data types can have up to 7 digits.

- **Double (double)** – A double type is the same as the float type with the primary difference of storing up to 16 digits. Unlike the float type, double denotes 64-bit double-precision floating points.

- **Long (long)** – Long is an integer data type (no decimal points) that may contain numbers from -9,223,372,036,854,775,808 to 9,223,372,036,854,775,807. This is the range of the 64-bit signed integers. Take note that for *int,* which denotes 32-bit signed integers, the range is from -2,147,483,648 to 2,147,483,647.

- **Short (short)** – In comparison to the long and int data types, the short data type denotes 16-bit signed integer types with a range from -32,768 to 32,767.

- **Sbyte** – The sbyte represents the smallest of the pack; denoting 8-bit signed integers which contain numbers from *-128* to *127*.

- **Byte, Uint, Ulong, Ushort** – These are the unsigned counterparts of the sbyte, int, long, and short value types. They *do not* contain numbers less than zero, which is why their entire range is extended to positive numbers. For byte, the range goes from 0 to 255. For uint, the range goes from 0 to *4,294,967,295*. For ulong, the range goes from 0 to *18,446,744,073,709,551,615*. And for ushort, the range goes from 0 to 65,535.

Going back to declaring variables, you can now declare them with specific data types using the keyword of said type. For example, if you want to declare the variable *x* with the data type *integer* without defining its value, you can use the following syntax:

```
int x;
```

Using this method, you may also declare multiple variables like:

```
int x, y, z;
```

Lastly, remember that you can still assign as a specific value for variables using this method of declaration. All you need to do is to use the assignment operator (=) and use the following syntax:

```
int x = 1, y = 2, z = 3;
```

Outputting Variables

The next thing to learn is how to use the values stored in variables with the output stream. For example, let us try using a variable for *pi* and use the `Console.WriteLine` function to print it in the application. Take a look at the example program below that is written for this simple purpose:

```
using System;

namespace Output

{

    class MainClass

    {

        public static void Main (string[]
args)

        {

            decimal pi;
            pi = 3.1416M;
            /* Remember that the default
values for the decimal data type contains the
suffix M */
            Console.WriteLine ("The value
of pi is " + pi);
            /* The operator + is used with
```

```
the Console.WriteLine method to use variable
values */

                    }

          }

}
```

Take note that the name *pi* is only used in the above program as an example. You can change the value assigned to the variable to anything you like and it will be printed with the `Console.WriteLine` method. Just remember that the decimal data type requires the suffix M to be valid.

Later on, you will learn how to perform operations with these variables. But in order to make those calculations matter; you should first learn how to utilize user input in setting the values for variables. Once you think you fully understand variables and data types, feel free to proceed to the next chapter.

Chapter 4 – All About User Input

In this Chapter:

**The Functions for Getting User Input*

**Saving User Input to Variables*

**Converting Data Types from User Input*

Understanding and learning how to use variables in a program is the first step to utilizing user input. Once these variables contain values, you can now perform various arithmetic and logical operations that will give your program a purpose. But first, let us discuss how to obtain values from user input.

How to Get User Input

The function `Console.ReadKey` briefly mentioned in the previous chapter is the simplest way to allow user interaction in the program. You can actually utilize user input using the following syntax:

```
ConsoleKeyInfo x;
```

```
/* ConsoleKeyInfo is a class that is used for
a single key press and can be used in
```

conjunction with modifier keys such as Alt, Ctrl, and Shift */

```
Console.WriteLine ("Press a letter\n");
```

/* The \n tells the program to write a new line */

```
x = Console.ReadKey ();
```

/* The program is now told to use Console.ReadKey for the variable x */

```
Console.Write ("\nYou pressed: ");

Console.WriteLine(x.Key.ToString());
```

/* Finally, the program is told to print the value of x, which was assigned using the Console.ReadKey function */

However, you need to learn a better method of obtaining user input and saving them to actual variables you can operate with. This time, you will need to use the Console.ReadLine function.

Using the Console.ReadLine Function

The purpose of this function is to tell the program to read the following *line* from the user input stream. You can use this function directly on an already-declared variable. However, you need to *convert* the data first so that it matches the variable.

For example, if you declare the string:

```
string MyString;
```

Then you need to use the function `Convert.ToString` in conjunction with the `Console.ReadLine` method to allow the ensuing user input to be stored to `MyString`.

Here is the proper syntax for using these methods:

```
string MyString;
MyString                =              Convert.ToString
(Console.ReadLine());
```

Here is an example of a program that accepts user input and prints it out as the *favorite color*.

```
using System;

namespace FavoriteColor

{

        class MainClass

        {
        public static void Main (string[] args)
```

```
{
    string MyString;

    /* The String is declared */
    Console.WriteLine ("Greetings! What
is your favorite color?");

    /* The user is asked for input */
    MyString =
Convert.ToString(Console.ReadLine());

    /* The input is converted to string
type and stored to the variable MyString
*/
    Console.WriteLine ("Your favorite
color is " + MyString);

    /* The program is told to output a
line in addition to the value stored in
MyString */

}

}

}
```

Converting to Other Data Types

As stated above, you need to convert the input obtained through the `Console.ReadLine` method into the appropriate data type before they can be stored to variables. There are specific syntaxes required for converting to data types. To serve as your guide, here is a list of the functions you need to use for specific data types which will be used primarily throughout the lessons in this book:

- **To Int** – `Convert.ToInt32`

- **To Decimal** – `Convert.ToDecimal`

- **To Char** – `Convert.ToChar`

- **To Bool** – `Convert.ToBoolean`

Chapter 5 – Performing Operations

In this Chapter:

**Introduction to the Basic Operators

**Performing Operators on Variables

**Using Logical Operators

At this point, you should now know how to write a program that allows user interaction in the simplest form. The user can now participate and have an influence on the course of the program. But something is still lacking. You need to give your program a *purpose*.

The Basic Operators of C#

C# uses operators that resemble the ones used in C++. There is a particularly large set of operators used in this programming language which are grouped across 15 categories:

- *Primary*

- *Unary*

- *Multiplicative*

- *Additive*

- *Relational and Type Testing*

- *Equality*

- *Shift*

- *Logical XOR*

- *Logical OR*

- *Logical AND*

- *Conditional AND*

- *Conditional OR*

- *Conditional*

- *Null-Coalescing*

- *Assignment and Lambda*

For beginners, you need to learn how to use the basic operators used for arithmetic and logical processes. These are the essential processes that will help breathe life into your program and give it an actual purpose.

Performing Mathematical Operations

Writing the methods and expressions that will perform operations is pretty self-explanatory. For example, if you want to add the values of variables x and y, you will be using the following syntax *after* the variables are declared and assigned values. You can print the resulting number directly using the `Console.Write` function with the following syntax:

```
Console.Write ("The sum is " + (x + y));
```

Remember that you need to enclose the arithmetic operation you want to perform in parentheses. Otherwise, the `Console.Write` function will understand the values of x and y merely as extensions of the line to be written. For example, if `x = 1` and `y = 2`, these will be the results:

```
Console.Write ("The sum is " + x + y); /* The
ensuing output will be The sum is 12 */
```

```
Console.Write ("The sum is " + (x + y)); /*
The ensuing output will be The sum is 3 */
```

Alternatively, you can store the resulting number into another variable. This way, you can prevent having to add + (x + y)); every time you want to print the sum of the two variables. Storing it to a separate variable will also allow you to use its value to perform further operations.

A Simple Calculator

The easiest way to experience how to create a fully-operational program in C# is by writing a small program that performs simple mathematical calculations. Using what you have learned about user input and variables, you should be able to obtain the values in which you are going to perform your operations on.

Here is an example program that will allow you to perform simple mathematical operations with two numbers:

```
using System;

namespace Calculator
{

    class MainClass
    {

    public static void Main (string[] args)
    {

    int x, y, a, b, c, d;
    Console.WriteLine ("Please insert the 1st
number.");
    x = Convert.ToInt32 (Console.ReadLine
());
    Console.WriteLine ("Please insert the 2nd
number.");
    y = Convert.ToInt32 (Console.ReadLine
());
    a = x + y; /* the sum of x and y is
stored to a */
    b = x - y; /* the difference is stored to
```

```
b */
    c = x * y; /* the product is stored to c
*/
    d = x / y; /*the quotient is stored to d
*/
    Console.WriteLine ("The sum of the 2
numbers: " + a);
    Console.WriteLine ("The difference is: "
+ b);
    Console.WriteLine ("The product is: " +
c);
    Console.WriteLine ("The quotient is: " +
d);
    Console.ReadKey ();

    }

    }

}
```

Other Operators

For the remaining chapters of this book, you will also be introduced to the other basic operators in C#. This includes the conditional, relational, and unary operators which can be used for creating loops. First, let us take a look at some of the useful *unary* operators:

Note: *The variable x is only used as an example to represent the operand and is not included in the operators itself.*

- **++x** – This operator will increase the numeric value of the operand by an increment of 1.

- **--x** – This operator will decrease the numeric value of the operand by a decrement of 1.

- **+x** – This operator simply denotes the value of the operand.

- **-x** – This operator will take the negative value of the operand.

Unary operators are named as such because they only affect the single operand they are attached to. These operators are useful for writing conditional statements and setting parameters for loops.

Another category of useful operators is the *relational* operators, which have the primary purpose of comparing two operands:

- **==** - This operator checks if the values of two operands equal each other.

- **!=** - As opposed to the == operator, this operator checks if the values of two operands are NOT equal.

- > - This operator checks if the value of the operand to the left is greater than the one on the right.

- < - This operator checks if the value of the operand to the left is less than the one on the righty

- >= - This operator checks if the operand to the left is greater than *or* equal to the one on the right.

- <= - This operator checks if the operand to the left is less than *or* equal to the one on the right.

Relational operators return a Boolean value and are used for creating conditional statements. They are also useful for setting conditional parameters when creating loops.

Lastly, conditional operators are basic operators that are used for checking two or more parameters. They return a Boolean value depending on the values of the operands. The two conditional operators are:

- **And (&&)** – This operator checks if *both* sides are true. If they are, it will result in the Boolean value for true.

- **Or (||)** – This operator checks if at least one of the sides is true. For example, the expression 1 < 2 || 1 > 2 will return the Boolean value true because the left side is true even though the right side is not.

Numbers Checker Program

You can take a look at the following example program that demonstrates how some of the operators under these 3 categories can be used. It is written specifically to fulfill the following:

- Ask for the input of a first number

- Ask for the input of a second number

- Checks to see if both numbers are the same

- Checks if the first number is smaller or bigger

- Checks if one of the numbers is negative

- Checks if one of the negative numbers is equal to -2

- Gets the increment of the first number

- Gets the decrement of the second number

Note: *Also notice that multiple flow control statements (if) will be used. These will be discussed in the next chapter.*

```
using System;


namespace Operations
{
```

```
class MainClass

{

public static void Main (string[] args)

{

int x, y;
Console.WriteLine ("Insert first
number.");
    x = Convert.ToInt32 (Console.ReadLine
());
    Console.WriteLine ("Insert second
number.");
    y = Convert.ToInt32 (console.ReadLine
());


    /* Relational Operators */

    if (x == y)
    {

        Console.WriteLine ("The two numbers
are equal.");

    }

    else if (x < y)
    {
```

```
Console.WriteLine ("The first number is
smaller.");

}

else
{

Console.WriteLine ("The first number is
bigger.");

}
```

/* Conditional Operators */

```
if (x < 0 || y <0)
{

        Console.WriteLine ("one of them is
negative.");

        if (x != -2 && y != -2)
        {

        Console.WriteLine ("None of them is
-2.");

        }

}
```

/* Unary Operators */

```
Console.WriteLine ("The increment of the
first number is " + ++x);

Console.WriteLine ("The decrement of the
second number is " + --y);

Console.ReadKey ();

    }

    }

}
```

Remember that you can use these operators to create *logic* within your program. These are essential for creating *flow control* statements, which will be discussed in the next chapter.

Chapter 6 – Flow Control in C#

In this Chapter:

**The Basics of If-Else Statements

**Using Switch Statements

**Generating Random Numbers

**Writing Loops

By now, you should notice that the programs you have written so far in C# run in one direction. They travel from the first line down to the last curly brace. You are also introduced to the *if-else* statements in the previous chapter, which will check for specific conditions before running methods. This is a single step in the right direction when it comes to understanding flow control in C# programs.

What is Flow Control?

In simple terms, you can use flow control statements to control the direction or *course* of your program. Instead of simply running each line and method from top to bottom, you may tell your program which specific ones to access at any given moment.

The if-else statement you used in the previous chapter is an example of flow control that uses Boolean logic. If one condition is met, then the following methods will be applied. To be clear, here is the proper syntax for writing if-else statements in C#:

```
if ("insert conditions here")
{

    /* Insert the methods you wish to run in case the conditions are met */

}

else if ("Insert secondary conditions here")
{

    /* If the first condition is not met, you can use else if to check for another condition and run other methods instead */

}

else
{

    /* You can run an else statement in case none of the prior if conditions are met; remember that else statements are optional */

}
```

Aside from the if-else statement, a simpler method of checking for specific conditions before running the appropriate result is using the *ternary operator* (?). With this operator, you can initialize the value of another variable depending on the returned Boolean value of the condition. The correct syntax for using this operator is as follows.

```
<condition> ? <result if true> : <result if
false>
```

For example, the if-else:

```
if (x != y)

    z = 1;

else


    z = 2;
```

Is the same as:

```
z = (x != y) ? 1 : 2;
```

In C# language, the practice of using conditional statements to control which lines of codes to run is also referred to as *branching*. Aside from using the ternary operator and if-else statements, you can control the course of your program using the *switch statement* and *loops*.

Switch

With the switch statement, you can write your program with different *cases* that trigger depending on the value of the variable in the *switch expression*. Here is what the switch statement looks like:

```
switch ("switch statement")
{

    case 1:
        /* Insert what will happen if the
switch statement variable equals 1 */
        break;

    case 2:
        /* Insert what will happen if the
switch statement variable equals 2 */
        break;

    default:
        /* Insert what will happen if the
switch statement variable does not equal any
of the case labels above */
        break;

}
```

Also bear in mind that you need to insert break; where you want to end the action in each case. Otherwise, the program will continue running through the rest of the cases and thus defeats the purpose of using the switch flow control statement.

Also take note that the `default` case is equivalent to the `else` statement in an if-else statement.

Here is a simple example that asks the user to insert a number from a given range and gives an appropriate response:

```
char x;
Console.WriteLine ("Insert a letter from
A-C".);
x = Convert.ToChar (Console.ReadLine ());
x = Char.ToUpper (x);

    switch (x)
    {

    case 'A':
    {

            Console.WriteLine ("You put
A.");

            break;

    }

    case 'B':
    {
```

```
            Console.WriteLine ("You put
B.");
            break;

        }

        case 'C':
        {

            Console.WriteLine ("You put
C.");
            break;

        }

        default:
        {

            Console.WriteLine ("Invalid
input.");
            break;

        }
```

Notice that for this example, the character input for variable x was converted to uppercase in the line x = Char.ToUpper (x);. With the switch statement shown above, remember that the cases only specifically check if the value of x is any of the uppercase characters *A, B*, and *C*.

If the user inputs lowercase *a* without converting it first to uppercase, the case statement will send the user to the `default` method. This is why you should always pay attention to the capitalization of letters, especially in variable names and `char` data types. Also be sure to encase character values in single quotation marks (') at all times.

Writing Loops

Another way to create variations on how your program will run is to use *loops*. A loop will basically keep on repeating the methods inside it as long as the required conditions are met. A loop also has a specific point wherein the condition is updated and rechecked. Once the condition required is no longer met, the loop stops and the application will resume.

There are three main types of loops:

While Loop

The while loops *tests* the condition first before running the enclosed statements. The simplest way to utilize a while loop is to create a program that counts down from 10. Here is how it is written:

```
int x = 10;

while (x > 0)
{

    Console.WriteLine (x);
    x--;

    /* In this example, the decrement
operator is used to prevent an infinite loop
*/

}
```

For Loop

The main difference between a for loop and a while loop is that the parameters for initializing, checking, and updating the prerequisite variable is included when declaring the for loop itself. The In relation to the example above, here is what a for loop would look like:

```
for (int x = 10; x > 0; x--)
{
```

```
Console.WriteLine (x);

}
```

Do-While Loop

The do-while loop runs the methods once before checking the condition. A convenient way to use this loop in a console application is to enclose the entire program in the loop, which will give the user the option to restart it.

To demonstrate the do-while loop, here is an example program that simulates the rolling of dice. Here are the things that this program will accomplish:

- Randomly generate two numbers from 1-6

- Get the total of the two numbers

- Ask the user in case he or she wants to roll again

Generating Random Numbers

To generate random numbers in C#, you need to call upon the random class, which can be used to generate instances of random numbers. It can be done using the *instance constructor* syntax which requires a name for the instance as well as optional parameters.

To create an instance of the random class, you can use the following syntax:

```
Random <"instance name"> = new Random ();
```

Additionally, you need variables that will actually put the random instance to use. For example, if you want to generate a random value for variable *random,* here is the syntax you need to use:

```
Random RandomInstance = new Random ();

int random = RandomInstance.Next (1, 101;
```

In this particular example, the random instance will generate a number from *1* to *100,* which is declared along with `RandomInstance`. Remember that the maximum value in the expression is always 1 more than the actual value. If you want, you can leave these parameters blank.

Without further ado, here is the die simulator program would look like:

```csharp
using System;

namespace DieRoller
{

    class MainClass
    {

    public static void Main (string[] args)
    {

    char Roll = 'R';

    /* First, we initialize the condition for
    the do-while loop */

    do {

    Random x = new Random ();

    /* We created an instance/object of the
    random class called 'x' */

    int die01 = x.Next (1, 7);
    Console.WriteLine ("The first die rolls
    "+ die01);

    /* The value of the first die or variable
    die01 is generated from 1-6 and printed */
```

```
    int die02 = x.Next (1, 7);
    Console.WriteLine ("The second die rolls
"+ die02);
```

/* The value of the second die or
variable *die02* is generated from 1-6 and
printed */

```
    Console.WriteLine ("You rolled " + (die01
+ die02));
```

/* The total value of both dice is
printed */

```
    Console.WriteLine ("Press R to Reroll");
    Roll = Convert.ToChar (Console.ReadLine
());
    Roll = Char.ToUpper (Roll);
```

/* Here, the user may press *R* to allow
the value of variable *Roll* to fulfill the
loop's condition */

```
    } while (Roll == 'R');
```

```
/* Finally, the program checks if the value of variable roll is still
Y and will restart if it is */
        }

}


}
```

Preview of my other books that might interest you:

HTML: Step by Step Beginners Guide to HTML

*The book "**HTML: Step by Step Beginners Guide to HTML**" will provide all essential information and training during the book which you'll need in order to upgrade your skills later with other languages and even with more sophisticated HTML.*

The reason why we start our "Learn Web Design" series with HTML is because he is the core to every website out there. No matter how basic or sophisticated one website is the HTML is always there and is essential for its existence.

In order to perfectly understand the material we'll go through everything from the absolute beginning. We'll do some exercises because the only way to master programming is by constant exercise and learning.

All the material in this book can be learned in less than a day but exercising and upgrading your skills later on is essential to becoming a good programmer.

You can check/download the book from <u>HERE</u>.

Java
Learn Java Programming with the Ultimate Crash Course for Beginners in no Time!

Today's applications are becoming increasingly powerful, especially with computers, smartphones, and tablets getting more processing power and memory every year. However, all of these devices are nothing without the operating system and programs they contain.

You might already be familiar with Java, whether it's from an introductory course in programming or a platform you had to install to make certain programs work on your computer, and that's not surprising at all since Java remains one of the most popular and in-demand programming languages in the world!

Despite the popularity of Java as a language and a platform, there remains still a shortage of qualified programmers to create meaningful and useful Java applications. Whether you're completely new to Java, or even to programming, or you feel that there's still a lot of room for improvement in terms of your current Java programming skills, this book will give you a strong foundation in both programming and Java.

If you're still wondering whether or not this book is for you, here are some statements to help you decide:

- You're a complete newbie and you need a book that introduces you gently to the world of programming
- You're already a Java developer but you'd like to sharpen your skills and create more efficient, error-free code
- You want to find a book that isn't overly technical but at the same time, not too dumbed-down
- You enjoy solving riddles and challenges
- You have a really good idea for a program and nobody has thought about it just yet
- You want to help people by creating programs that they need but can't seem to find

If you can identify with any of these statements, then you've come to the right place. This book provides a self-paced comprehensive crash course in Java, from the very definition of programming to the most advanced topics in Java. This book will provide plenty of source codes for you to play and experiment with in order to help you understand Java better. After finishing this book, you should be able to create Java programs confidently.

This book can serve as both a reference and a walkthrough in Java, so feel free to skip and skim through chapters that talk about things you're already well acquainted with and jump back and forth between chapters if that works better for you.

Conclusion

Thank you again for downloading this book!

I hope this book was able to help you to learn the basics of programming with C#!

The next step is to keep on learning! Remember that you have much more to learn about the amazing world of C#.

Finally, if you enjoyed this book, then I'd like to ask you for a favor, would you be kind enough to leave a review for this book on Amazon? It'd be greatly appreciated!

Click here to leave a review for this book on Amazon!

Thank you and good luck!